PRESIDENTS

JAMES A. GARFIELD

A MyReportLinks.com Book

Jeff C. Young

MyReportLinks.com Books

an imprint of

 Enslow Publishers, Inc.

Box 398, 40 Industrial Road
Berkeley Heights, NJ 07922
USA

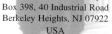

To Frank J. Petrella, Omicron '70, a brother in the truest and finest sense of the word.

MyReportLinks.com Books, an imprint of Enslow Publishers, Inc. MyReportLinks is a trademark of Enslow Publishers, Inc.

Library of Congress Cataloging-in-Publication Data

Young, Jeff C., 1948–
    James A. Garfield / Jeff C. Young.
       p. cm. — (Presidents)
    Summary: A biography of the twentieth president of the United States, whose term was cut short when he was fatally wounded a few months after his inauguration. Includes Internet links to Web sites, source documents, and photographs related to James Garfield.
    Includes bibliographical references and index.
    ISBN 0-7660-5100-5
    1. Garfield, James A. (James Abram), 1831–1881—Juvenile literature. 2. Presidents—United States—Biography—Juvenile literature. [1. Garfield, James A. (James Abram), 1831–1881. 2. Presidents.] I. Title. II. Series.
    E687.Y68 2003
    973.8'4'092—dc21

                                            2002008994

Printed in the United States of America

10 9 8 7 6 5 4 3 2 1

Photo Credits: © Corel Corporation, pp. 1 (background), 3; Biographical Directory of the United States Congress, p. 41; Department of the Interior, p. 40; Dover Publications, Inc., p. 1; eHistory.com, p. 25; Georgetown University, p. 43; Grolier Encyclopedia, pp. 32, 34; HarpWeek, p. 22; Hiram College Archives, pp. 18, 29; Library of Congress, pp. 12, 36, 38; Middle Creek National Battlefield, p. 27; MyReportLinks.com Books, p. 4; National Archives and Records Administration, p. 24; The American President, p. 15; Western Reserve Historical Society, pp. 19, 39.

Cover Photo: © Corel Corporation; Library of Congress.

Contents

MyReportLinks.com Books
Great Books, Great Links, Great for Research!

MyReportLinks.com Books present the information you need to learn about your report subject. In addition, they show you where to go on the Internet for more information. The pre-evaluated Report Links that back up this book are kept up to date on **www.myreportlinks.com**. With the purchase of a MyReportLinks.com Books title, you and your library gain access to the Report Links that specifically back up that book. The Report Links save hours of research time and link to dozens—even hundreds—of Web sites, source documents, and photos related to your report topic.

Please see "To Our Readers" on the Copyright page for important information about this book, the MyReportLinks.com Books Web site, and the Report Links that back up this book.

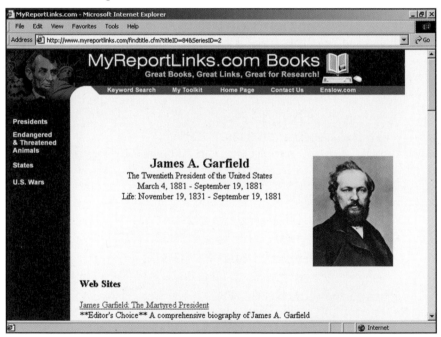

Access:

The Publisher will provide access to the Report Links that back up this book and will try to keep these Report Links up to date on our Web site for three years from the book's first publication date. Please enter **PGA2212** if asked for a password.

Report Links

The Internet sites described below can be accessed at
http://www.myreportlinks.com

*EDITOR'S CHOICE

▶ **James Garfield: The Martyred President**

At this PBS site you will learn about James A. Garfield's life before, during, and after his presidency. You will also learn about his presidential campaign, family life, death, and legacy.

Link to this Internet site from http://www.myreportlinks.com

*EDITOR'S CHOICE

▶ **Objects From the Presidency**

By navigating through this site you will find objects related to all of the United States presidents, including James A. Garfield. You will also find illustrations of his assassination, inauguration, and a photograph of the tile that he fell upon after being shot.

Link to this Internet site from http://www.myreportlinks.com

*EDITOR'S CHOICE

▶ **"I Do Solemnly Swear . . ."**

At this Web site you can experience James A. Garfield's inauguration through images and documents including diary entries and a portion of his inaugural address.

Link to this Internet site from http://www.myreportlinks.com

*EDITOR'S CHOICE

▶ **James A. Garfield National Historic Site**

Here you can take a virtual tour of Lawnfield, the James A. Garfield National Historic Site. You can also read a biography of James and Lucretia Garfield, learn about their relationship, and view pictures of their family.

Link to this Internet site from http://www.myreportlinks.com

*EDITOR'S CHOICE

▶ **The American Presidency: James A. Garfield Biography**

In this biography you will learn about James A. Garfield's early life, Civil War service, congressional career, and presidency. You will also find "fun facts" and the complete text of his inaugural address.

Link to this Internet site from http://www.myreportlinks.com

*EDITOR'S CHOICE

▶ **IPL Potus: James Abram Garfield**

Here you will find a brief overview of James A. Garfield through personal data, election results, cabinet members, and notable events of his presidency. You will also find points of interest, his inaugural address, and additional Internet resources.

Link to this Internet site from http://www.myreportlinks.com

 The Internet sites described below can be accessed at
http://www.myreportlinks.com

▶ The Assassination of James A. Garfield

At this Web site you will find newspaper accounts of James A. Garfield's assassination, a collection of poetry written about the assassination, and a map of the train station where Garfield was assassinated.

Link to this Internet site from http://www.myreportlinks.com

▶ American Presidents—Life Portraits: James A. Garfield

This Web site includes basic facts about James A. Garfield's life and presidency. You will also find a letter written by Garfield to his wife.

Link to this Internet site from http://www.myreportlinks.com

▶ Background on the Pendleton Act

The text of the Pendleton Act can be found at this Web site. This act, which came into being after Garfield was assassinated by a disappointed office seeker, reformed the system of political patronage.

Link to this Internet site from http://www.myreportlinks.com

▶ Battle of Chickamauga

At this Web site you will find an in-depth description of the Battle of Chickamauga, in which Garfield earned the title of major general. You will also learn about the events leading up to the battle, the battle itself, and the outcome.

Link to this Internet site from http://www.myreportlinks.com

▶ Blaine, James Gillespie

Here you will find a brief biography of James G. Blaine, Garfield's secretary of state, who was with the president when he was assassinated. Blaine was also Speaker of the House, a senator, and a Republican presidential nominee.

Link to this Internet site from http://www.myreportlinks.com

▶ Charles Guiteau Collection

At this Web site you will find documents written by Charles Guiteau, the man who assassinated James Garfield. The writings include a speech supporting Garfield's election, letters by Guiteau explaining his actions to William T. Sherman and the American people, and an account of the assassination.

Link to this Internet site from http://www.myreportlinks.com

Report Links

 The Internet sites described below can be accessed at
http://www.myreportlinks.com

▶ **The Death Of President Garfield, 1881**
Beginning with Garfield's assassination and ending with his death, this
article focuses on the final months of President James A. Garfield's life.

Link to this Internet site from http://www.myreportlinks.com

▶ **HarpWeek: Presidential Elections, 1880**
HarpWeek provides a comprehensive overview of the Democratic and
Republican conventions of 1880. Here you will find election results,
essays on the key issues of the campaign, biographies of the key players,
and dozens of political cartoons.

Link to this Internet site from http://www.myreportlinks.com

▶ **History Buff—Alexander Graham Bell and
the Garfield Assassination**
Here you will find an article about Alexander Graham Bell's attempt
to find the lost bullet lodged in Garfield. Bell used a device whose
technology was based on that of the telephone, his new invention.

Link to this Internet site from http://www.myreportlinks.com

▶ **James A. Garfield: Inaugural Address**
At this Web site you can read the full text of James A. Garfield's
inaugural address, given on Friday, March 4, 1881.

Link to this Internet site from http://www.myreportlinks.com

▶ **James A. Garfield: Slumbering Thunder**
In this brief article about James A. Garfield, you will learn about his
politics, religion, and philosophy of life. You will also find a letter from
Garfield to his mother, a video clip about his challenge to "senatorial
courtesy," and many helpful links.

Link to this Internet site from http://www.myreportlinks.com

▶ **James Garfield's Obituary**
Read the obituary of James A. Garfield, which includes an account of
his last moments, the first news of his death, and an account of Vice
President Chester A. Arthur taking the presidential oath.

Link to this Internet site from http://www.myreportlinks.com

Report Links

The Internet sites described below can be accessed at
http://www.myreportlinks.com

▶ **May 16, 1881—Both New York Senators Resign**
Here you will find out why James Garfield's appointment of William H.
Robertson for collector of the Port of New York caused the resignations
of Senators Roscoe Conkling and Thomas Platt.

Link to this Internet site from http://www.myreportlinks.com

▶ **Middle Creek National Battlefield: The Historic Battle**
This site includes an article about the Civil War battle known as the Battle
of Middle Creek, which established Garfield's reputation as a soldier.

Link to this Internet site from http://www.myreportlinks.com

▶ **National Museum of Health and Medicine Anatifacts: President
James Garfield's Vertebrae**
At this Web site you can read an article about the medical complications that
led to the death of James A. Garfield. You will also find a model of the
president's spine illustrating the path of the bullet and a diagram of the injury.

Link to this Internet site from http://www.myreportlinks.com

▶ **On This Day: June 7, 1873**
In addition to an 1873 political cartoon by C. S. Reinhart, you will find an
article about one of the two biggest controversies of Garfield's congressional
career—the pay raise Congress voted for itself, which became known as the
"salary grab."

Link to this Internet site from http://www.myreportlinks.com

▶ **On This Day: March 15, 1873**
Featured at this Web site is Thomas Nast's 1873 editorial cartoon of
the Crédit Mobilier scandal, a scandal that nearly cost James A. Garfield
his career.

Link to this Internet site from http://www.myreportlinks.com

▶ **On This Day: March 25, 1882**
Here you will find an article, supplemented with a cartoon by Thomas
Nast, about the Star Route scandal, one of the first events in the brief
Garfield presidency.

Link to this Internet site from http://www.myreportlinks.com

Report Links

 The Internet sites described below can be accessed at
http://www.myreportlinks.com

▶ President James Abram Garfield

At this Web site you will find a brief biography of James A. Garfield.
You will also find a list of notable events during his presidency, a list
of his cabinet members, and additional Internet resources.

Link to this Internet site from http://www.myreportlinks.com

▶ Robert Todd Lincoln (1843–1926)

Here you will find a brief biography of Garfield's secretary of war,
Robert Todd Lincoln, who was present at his assassination.

Link to this Internet site from http://www.myreportlinks.com

▶ Sarah Orne Jewett, "The Plea of Insanity"

Here you will find an essay on the trial of Charles Guiteau for the
murder of James A. Garfield. An explanation of the historical context
in which the essay was written and excerpts from newspapers and
magazines covering the trial are included.

Link to this Internet site from http://www.myreportlinks.com

▶ U.S. Senate Historical Minutes: Senate Service Record Set

This article cxamines the 1880 Republican convention in which
Garfield supported Senator John Sherman but ultimately became
his party's nominee for president.

Link to this Internet site from http://www.myreportlinks.com

▶ The White House: James A. Garfield

This White House biography of James A. Garfield focuses on Garfield's
battle with New York Senator Roscoe Conkling over William H.
Robertson's appointment as head of the New York Customs House.

Link to this Internet site from http://www.myreportlinks.com

▶ The White House: Lucretia Rudolph Garfield

At the official White House Web site, you will find the biography
of First Lady Lucretia Rudolph Garfield. The story of how she met
James A. Garfield is included.

Link to this Internet site from http://www.myreportlinks.com

Highlights

1831—*Nov. 19:* Born in Orange, Ohio, southeast of Cleveland.

1848—Leaves home to earn a living working on a canal boat.

1849–1852—Attends school at Geauga Seminary and the Western Reserve Eclectic Institute (later Hiram College) and also works as a teacher.

1854–1856—Attends and graduates with honors from Williams College in Williamstown, Massachusetts.

1856–1857—Serves as a professor of Greek, Latin, and literature at Hiram College.

1857–1861—Serves as president of Hiram College.

1858—*Nov. 11:* Marries Lucretia (Crete) Rudolph, his boyhood sweetheart.

1859—Elected to the Ohio State Senate.

1860—Completes law studies and is admitted to the Ohio bar.

1861–1863—Joins the Ohio Volunteer Infantry and serves with the Ohio Forty-second Regiment in the Civil War. Rises in rank from lieutenant colonel to major general.

1863–1880—Serves in the U.S. House of Representatives.

1880—Elected to the U.S. Senate but declines seat after he is elected twentieth president of the United States.

1881—*March 4:* Inaugurated as president.

July 2: Shot and mortally wounded by Charles Guiteau.

Sept. 19: President James A. Garfield dies.

Chapter 1

Fighting for His Life, 1881

If President James Garfield heard the footsteps behind him, he paid no attention to them. There were many other sounds in Washington's busy Baltimore and Potomac Railroad Station on the morning of July 2, 1881. The recently inaugurated president was walking and talking with his secretary of state, James G. Blaine.

Their conversation was abruptly interrupted by the sharp sound of a single gunshot. Almost instantly, President Garfield felt a sharp, burning pain. In response, he straightened up and threw his head back. He was dazed, but still standing. A second shot caused the president to throw up his hands and cry: "My God! What is that?"[1]

Then he fell to his knees. Garfield was conscious, but he appeared to be in shock. His pulse was faint and his breathing was shallow and labored. His face was pale. Although he was covered in sweat, he complained that his legs and feet were cold.

A mattress was quickly brought in from a sleeping car. The gravely wounded president was then carried up some stairs into a large empty room. The first physician to arrive gave the president some stimulants to keep his heart beating. About fifteen to twenty minutes later, a second doctor arrived. He found one bullet, which had merely grazed President Garfield's arm. He could not find the second bullet. He poked and probed with unwashed fingers and medical instruments. The poking and probing are what probably caused the wound to get infected.

Soon, there was a team of doctors tending to the stricken president. They concluded that the missing bullet had penetrated some internal organ. There was little hope for recovery. President Garfield seemed to sense it. When one doctor tried to cheer him up, Garfield told him, "I thank you doctor, but I am a dead man."[2]

At one point, there were nearly twenty doctors milling about. All suggested various remedies, but no one took charge. Finally, Garfield asked to be taken to the White House. That was one thing the doctors were able to agree on.

After being taken to the White House, he lay in bed and heard the doctors hovering around him say, "He is dying."[3] The doctors also said that they believed he would not "live out the hour."[4]

▲ On July 2, 1881, less than four months after he was inaugurated president, James A. Garfield was shot by an assassin in a Washington, D.C., train station. This depiction of the shooting appeared in an illustrated newspaper on July 16, 1881.

Members of President Garfield's family were notified of the attempted assassination. His wife, Lucretia, arrived that evening. She assured her husband that she would nurse him back to health. When he spoke of death, she cut him off.

For a time, it seemed that Lucretia was right. Daily bulletins issued by the team of doctors were hopeful, but misleading. From July 5 to July 23, President Garfield seemed to be recovering. But after that, it became apparent that the infection was spreading. Alexander Graham Bell tried unsuccessfully to locate the second bullet, using a metal detector he invented. Everyone seemed unaware that the president's bed had metal springs. This, of course, made the metal detector useless.[5] At that time, medical science did not yet have the benefit of X-rays for viewing internal organs or locating objects such as lodged bullets. Also, antibiotics would not be available until many years later.

On September 6, the president was moved by train from the White House to an oceanside cottage in Elberon, New Jersey. Once again, the president seemed to be getting stronger. When he was propped up before an open window with a view of the ocean, Garfield said, "This is delightful . . . I am myself again."[6]

By mid-September, there was no more talk of a recovery. Garfield's chills, fever, and vomiting resumed. On September 19, the president's temperature rose to 108.8 degrees. That evening, Garfield spoke his last words, to his chief of staff, David G. Swaim: "Swaim, can't you stop this [pain]? Oh, Swaim!"[7]

After bravely fighting death for eighty days, the life and brief administration of James A. Garfield came to an end.

Chapter 2

The Early Years, 1831–1858

James A. Garfield was born in the village of Orange in Cuyahoga County, Ohio, on November 19, 1831. He was the last president to be born in a log cabin. James was an unusually large baby. He weighed ten pounds at birth. His mother, Eliza, called him "the largest Babe I ever had."[1]

James was only eighteen months old when his father, Abram, died. Abram had been battling a forest fire, which threatened his crops. He was nearly exhausted and chilled to the bone before the flames were subdued. It is believed that he died of pneumonia.

Eliza was left to raise four children. She sold fifty acres of their farm, and with the help of friends and relatives, she farmed the remaining thirty acres. James was the youngest child, and since he was the "baby" of the family, he received the most attention.

▶ A Gifted Child

Eliza Garfield believed that her son James was destined for greatness. The feeling grew stronger when she saw that James was an uncommonly bright child. He began walking at nine months. At ten months, he was climbing ladders. James started reading when he was only three years old.

Eliza decided that James would be the one child to receive an education. She donated some land so that a log cabin school could be built close to the family farm. James's early education was limited, but concentrated. He studied spelling, arithmetic, and grammar. There were few books available, so James read them intently. He practically memorized their contents.

When he was twelve, James began working after school. He helped neighbors with planting, harvesting, and other farm chores. James was not a very good worker. He was clumsy and he tended to daydream. Sometimes, when chopping wood, he would cut himself with the ax.

James's love of reading made him restless and eager to travel to faraway places. He loved reading sea stories and dreamed of becoming a sailor. When he had time to himself, James would frequent the wharves of Cleveland and run errands for the canal boat captains. He would listen

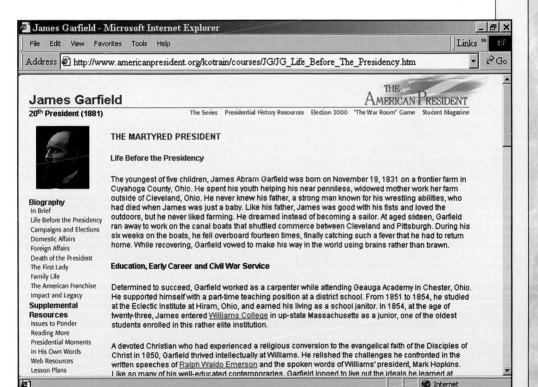

James Garfield, the last U.S. president to be born in a log cabin, grew up in humble surroundings in frontier Ohio.

to their tales of travel and adventure and yearn to go with them.

Canal Boat Driver

James quit school to go after his dream. At sixteen, he hiked to the Cleveland waterfront and tried to find work on one of the sailing ships or steamers. After being turned away, James found work on a canal boat as a driver. He drove the horses or mules that towed the boat through the water. It was boring work. James would walk along the towpath—a path alongside the canal—poking the animals with a stick to keep them moving.

James worked on the canal for six weeks. During that time, he was fished out of the water more than a dozen times. Falling overboard was a serious problem for someone who could not swim. He became ill, most likely with malaria, and returned home. It took him several months to recover.

While bedridden, James gradually lost his desire to be a sailor. He did a lot of reading, and his mother convinced him to return to school. In the spring of 1849, James enrolled at Geauga Seminary in Chester, Ohio.

The Young Teacher

After finishing the spring term at Geauga, James returned home to work. He spent the summer working as a carpenter and as a farmhand. Another year of study at Geauga qualified James to take the state tests for a teacher's certificate. He became certified and started teaching school when he was only eighteen. James's first teaching job paid him $13 a month plus room and board.

In the spring of 1850, James returned to Geauga. He took classes in Latin, botany, and algebra. Around October

1850, James left the school because of religious differences. He had recently been baptized into the Disciples of Christ faith. Baptists had founded Geauga, and James could not accept all of their beliefs.

▶ Latin and Greek Scholar

In the fall of 1851, James entered the Western Reserve Eclectic Institute (now called Hiram College) in Hiram, Ohio. He chose the school because it was run by the Disciples of Christ. James worked his way through school by teaching and sometimes working as a janitor. After a full day of teaching, going to classes, and studying, James would go to bed at 11:00 P.M.

James worked and studied hard. He learned to read books in both Latin and Greek. He was so absorbed in his teaching and studies that he had no interest in politics. During the presidential campaign of 1852, James wrote that he was glad he was not old enough to vote because he detested politics and politicians.

▶ Scholar and Public Speaker

In autumn of 1854, James enrolled at Williams College in Williamstown, Massachusetts, as a junior. He blossomed as a scholar and as a public speaker and became the star of the school's debate team. He was also the editor of the school's literary magazine. His experiences with the debate team led him to take an interest in politics. He found himself supporting the recently formed Republican Party.

James graduated from Williams College with honors in 1856. Like many new college graduates, he was still unsure about a career choice. He thought about becoming a preacher, but he settled on teaching. Politics was still a passing interest.

▲ *James Garfield returned to the Western Reserve Eclectic Institute (known today as Hiram College) to teach the classics and English grammar. This photograph of him was taken in 1856.*

▶ Hiram College: Teacher and President

James returned to Ohio after graduation. He needed to find employment because he had become engaged before graduating from Williams. He first met his fiancée, Lucretia Rudolph, when they were classmates at Geauga Seminary. Crete, as James called her, was well educated, and she was also a teacher.

His first job was at his alma mater, Western Reserve Eclectic Institute in Hiram, Ohio. He taught Latin, Greek, and English grammar and was well liked and respected by his students. James Garfield was not really happy teaching there, however.

The school's president was often absent and was very lax in supervising the faculty and students. The school was also having financial problems. Garfield planned to leave when his one-year contract ended. "Had I known before all I now know," he said, "I would not have come here at all."[2]

In May 1857, the school's board of trustees forced the president to retire. They chose Garfield, who was only

▲ On November 11, 1858, after a four-year-long engagement, Lucretia Rudolph and James A. Garfield were married at the home of the bride's parents, in Hiram, Ohio.

twenty-six, to succeed him. Despite the promotion and increased responsibilities, James Garfield still had the same teaching load and no pay increase. There were also other demands on his time.

He was an ordained minister in the Disciples of Christ. He preached almost every Sunday. He also lectured on literary and scientific subjects.

▶ New Beginnings

After four years of being engaged, James Garfield and Lucretia Rudolph were wed on November 11, 1858. Along with teaching, preaching, and being a husband, Garfield also began studying law. He was becoming more interested in politics and less interested in being a teacher and clergyman. He expressed his restlessness in a letter written to a friend: "My heart will never be satisfied to spend my life in teaching. I think there are other fields in which a man can do more."[3] Soon, politics would become one of those fields for James Garfield.

Chapter 3 ▶

Politician and Legislator, 1859–1861

In 1859, a committee of Ohio Republicans asked Garfield to run for the state senate. He was picked over three other men as the Republican candidate for state senator. Church leaders were unhappy with Garfield's decision to enter politics. He blunted their objections by pointing out that he had not actively sought the nomination. Garfield convinced them that he could be a politician and a legislator without compromising his religious beliefs.

Garfield Takes a Stand

While campaigning, Garfield was forced to take a stand on slavery. At Oberlin, Ohio, a large and angry group of abolitionists—people who wanted to abolish slavery—tried to keep federal marshals from enforcing the Fugitive Slave Act. The act, a federal law, provided reward money for the arrest and return of escaped slaves. The abolitionists had forcibly removed an escaped slave from the custody of federal marshals.

The abolitionists received prison sentences for violating the Fugitive Slave Act, and the Ohio Supreme Court upheld their convictions. Their plight became a campaign issue. Although Garfield disliked the Fugitive Slave Act, he believed that the judges were bound by law to make the decision they did, and he supported it.

First-Term Lawmaker

Garfield's stand cost him the support of abolitionists in the Republican Party, but he still won election to the

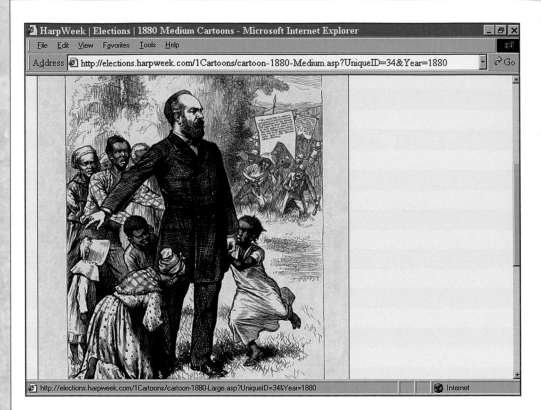

▲ *This 1880 political cartoon shows Garfield, then the Republican presidential candidate, as the protector of black Americans to an idealized extent.*

Ohio state legislature. At the age of twenty-eight, he became the youngest member of the Ohio General Assembly.

First-term lawmakers were expected to listen and learn, not to make speeches. Garfield was willing to do that until a bill threatened to cut funds for school libraries. Garfield, the book lover, spoke out against it, and his speaking skills earned him the respect of his colleagues.

▶ Matters at Home

In the spring of 1860, when the General Assembly adjourned, Garfield returned to work at the Eclectic Institute.

The school had run smoothly while Garfield was away. The same could not be said for his personal life. When he stayed in Columbus, Ohio's capital and seat of government, Garfield discouraged Crete from visiting. He claimed that legislative business kept him too busy to devote much time to her.

He even told her that he thought their marriage was "a great mistake."[1] The birth of their first child, a daughter they named Eliza, did not bring them any closer together. The day after she was born, Garfield was away making a Fourth of July speech.

Thirteen years later, Garfield would write that he and Crete had come to understand each other and referred to the "beautiful results we . . . are now enjoying."[2] James and Crete would have seven children. Two, including their first child, would die as infants. The others—Mary, Harry, James, Irvin, and Abram—would be dearly loved and enjoyed by their parents.

▶ Campaigning for Lincoln

During the presidential campaign of 1860, Garfield gave more than fifty speeches supporting the Republican presidential candidate, Abraham Lincoln. James Garfield truly blossomed as an orator. Crowds were moved and persuaded by his forceful and eloquent speaking style.

Ohio newspapers began calling him "a rising man."[3] Even the Democratic newspapers grudgingly took note of his speaking talents. They wrote, "He presented the doctrines of his party in a straightforward manner, and aside from some ingenious reasoning in support of them made a very good speech."[4]

On November 6, 1860, Garfield was delighted to see that his hard work had paid off. Abraham Lincoln carried

Ohio and enough other states to win the presidential election. But before Lincoln was inaugurated, seven Southern states had seceded and formed the Confederate States of America. In Washington, Congress was futilely looking for a compromise solution.

Garfield harbored no hopes for a compromise. He thought civil war was inevitable. He thought nothing "this side of a miracle of God"[5] could prevent it. He accepted the war as necessary to save the Union, and he believed a Union victory over the Confederacy would forever end slavery in America.

Soon, Garfield would leave his family, his college presidency, and his political career to fight for those very things.

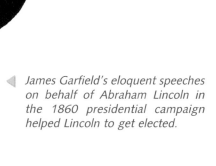

James Garfield's eloquent speeches on behalf of Abraham Lincoln in the 1860 presidential campaign helped Lincoln to get elected.

Chapter 4 ▶

A Talented Union Officer, 1861–1863

On April 12, 1861, Garfield was sitting in the state senate chamber when one of his colleagues burst in. The senator was waving a telegram. Then he shouted, "Mr. President, the telegraph announces that the secessionists are bombarding Fort Sumter!"[1] Fort Sumter was located about six miles outside of Charleston, South Carolina. The

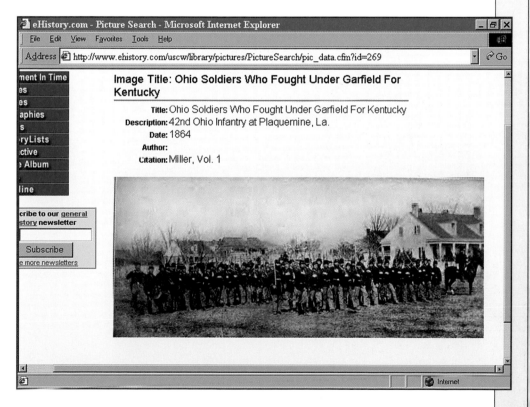

eHistory.com - Picture Search - Microsoft Internet Explorer

File   Edit   View   Favorites   Tools   Help

Address http://www.ehistory.com/uscw/library/pictures/PictureSearch/pic_data.cfm?id=269   Go

ment In Time
es
es
aphies
s
ryLists
ctive
e Album

line

cribe to our general
story newsletter

Subscribe
e more newsletters

Image Title: Ohio Soldiers Who Fought Under Garfield For Kentucky

Title: Ohio Soldiers Who Fought Under Garfield For Kentucky
Description: 42nd Ohio Infantry at Plaquemine, La.
Date: 1864
Author:
Citation: Miller, Vol. 1

Internet

▲ *Garfield was in charge of the Forty-second Ohio Infantry.*

fort was occupied by federal troops. The attack on it by the Confederacy amounted to an act of war.

Initial Setback

Garfield was ready to go to war. For the past several months, he had been reading biographies of military leaders and dozens of books on military strategy and history. With the quiet backing of Governor William Dennison of Ohio, Garfield tried to get a commission as a colonel in the Seventh Regiment of the Ohio Volunteer Infantry. The soldiers voted and chose a militiaman named Erastus B. Tyler as their colonel. Garfield was humiliated and depressed by their rejection. It was, however, the last time that he would lose an election.

Colonel Garfield

In June 1861, Governor Dennison offered Garfield an appointment as a lieutenant colonel of another Ohio regiment. Garfield turned it down. In August 1861, he changed his mind and became a lieutenant colonel with the Forty-second Ohio Volunteer Infantry. A few weeks later, the governor promoted him to the rank of colonel.

The first thing that Colonel Garfield had to do was recruit soldiers for his regiment. He began by getting students and graduates of the Eclectic Institute to enlist. By late November, his regiment numbered one thousand men. About two weeks later, the hastily assembled unit was called to active duty.

Military Leader and Tactician

The orders that Garfield received separated him from the Forty-second Ohio Infantry. They went to Catlettsburg, Kentucky, and Garfield went to Louisville. Confederate

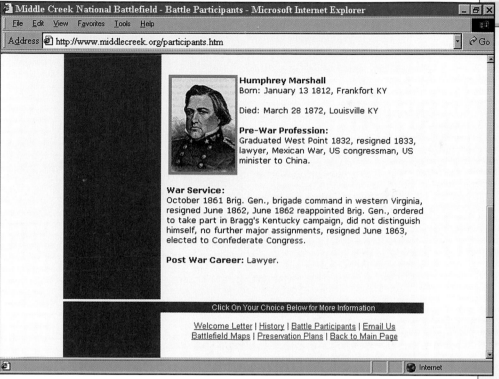

Middle Creek National Battlefield - Battle Participants - Microsoft Internet Explorer

File   Edit   View   Favorites   Tools   Help

Address http://www.middlecreek.org/participants.htm

Humphrey Marshall
Born: January 13 1812, Frankfort KY

Died: March 28 1872, Louisville KY

Pre-War Profession:
Graduated West Point 1832, resigned 1833,
lawyer, Mexican War, US congressman, US
minister to China.

War Service:
October 1861 Brig. Gen., brigade command in western Virginia,
resigned June 1862, June 1862 reappointed Brig. Gen., ordered
to take part in Bragg's Kentucky campaign, did not distinguish
himself, no further major assignments, resigned June 1863,
elected to Confederate Congress.

Post War Career: Lawyer.

Click On Your Choice Below for More Information

Welcome Letter | History | Battle Participants | Email Us
Battlefield Maps | Preservation Plans | Back to Main Page

Internet

▲ General Humphrey Marshall was the Confederate leader whom
Garfield defeated in the Battle of Middle Creek.

troops under the command of General Humphrey
Marshall were advancing toward southeastern Kentucky.
The advancing army was a threat to the left flank of Union
troops commanded by General Don Carlos Buell.

Buell wanted his army to march south to Nashville,
Tennessee, and capture the city. But first, Marshall's forces
had to be driven back. General Buell asked Colonel
Garfield to work out a tactic, or battle plan, for driving
Marshall away. The next morning, Garfield explained
his tactic to General Buell. Although it was a daring and

dangerous plan, Buell put his trust in Garfield and approved the plan with a few minor changes.

Battle of Middle Creek

The battle plan called for Garfield's troops to rout the Confederate forces from Paintsville, Kentucky, and join forces with Colonel Jonathan Cranor's army. Marshall's forces retreated once, avoiding Garfield's army, and then retreated again to escape Cranor's army. Garfield and his men finally engaged the enemy at the Battle of Middle Creek on January 10, 1862. It was a minor battle, with few casualties, but it accomplished its goal: It drove Marshall's forces out of eastern Kentucky. Middle Creek also established Garfield's reputation as an able military leader and tactician, and he was promoted in rank to brigadier general.

In April 1862, General Garfield and his men fought in the Battle of Shiloh. However, they arrived on the second day, when the battle was almost over. The only fighting they saw was a brief skirmish with the retreating Confederate cavalry.

Congress Beckons

By the summer of 1862, Garfield had lost much of his zest for the military life. He let his friends know he was available to run for Congress. On September 2, 1862, at the district Republican convention held in Garrettsville, Ohio, Garfield was nominated as the Republican candidate. In October, he defeated his Democratic opponent, D. B. Woods, by a margin of almost two to one.

Despite being elected to Congress, Garfield did not immediately leave the army. Congress would not begin its next session until December 1863. After recovering from dysentery, Garfield reported to Washington, D.C., to await his next military assignment. He was kept waiting several weeks before being assigned to serve under General William S. Rosecrans.

▶ A War Hero Resigns

Under Rosecrans, Garfield hoped to command a division. He wanted to lead troops in a major battle. Instead Rosecrans made him his chief of staff. Garfield became a trusted confidant and military advisor to General Rosecrans.

▲ *At the beginning of the Civil War, Garfield was a lieutenant colonel. After leading the Union army to a victory at the Battle of Middle Creek in January 1862, he was promoted to brigadier general.*

During the summer of 1863, Garfield planned the capture of Chattanooga, Tennessee.[2] In September 1863, at the Battle of Chickamauga, in Georgia, Garfield distinguished himself for bravery under fire. After General Rosecrans was forced to retreat, Garfield rode to join General George H. Thomas and his men. They were engaged in some of the battle's heaviest fighting. Garfield helped them hold off the advancing Confederate troops. His bravery earned him a promotion to the rank of major (two-star) general.

Two months later, Garfield met with President Lincoln and asked Lincoln if he should stay in the army or take his seat in Congress. Lincoln told Garfield that he had plenty of generals but few congressmen with practical military knowledge and experience. That convinced Garfield to resign his military commission.

In December 1863, Garfield took his seat in the U.S. House of Representatives. For the next seventeen years, the House would be Garfield's home.

Chapter 5 ▶

Congressman Garfield, 1863–1880

On December 7, 1863, Garfield was sworn in as a member of the House of Representatives in the Thirty-eighth Congress. He was appointed to the Military Affairs Committee and quickly became a favorite of the committee chairman, Representative Robert Schenck. Schenck and Garfield were both from Ohio, and both had served as generals in the Union army. Schenck taught Garfield the ins and outs of getting bills passed.

As a member of the Military Affairs Committee, Garfield aligned himself with a faction known as the Radical Republicans. They were the most outspoken critics of Lincoln's war policies. After the Civil War, Garfield and other Radical Republicans called for harsh policies against the defeated Confederacy.

In his first speech in the House, Garfield strongly supported a bill that called for the seizure of rebel property. He declared, "I hold it as a settled truth that the leaders of this rebellion can never live in peace in this republic."[1] Garfield believed that the leaders of the Confederacy should be imprisoned, executed, or deported from America.

▶ Garfield, a Radical Republican

After Abraham Lincoln was shot on April 14, 1865, and died the following day, Vice President Andrew Johnson became president. At first, Garfield supported Johnson's lenient policies toward the defeated South. He even tried to act as a liaison between the new president and the

Back   Forward   Stop   Review   Home   Explore   Favorites   History

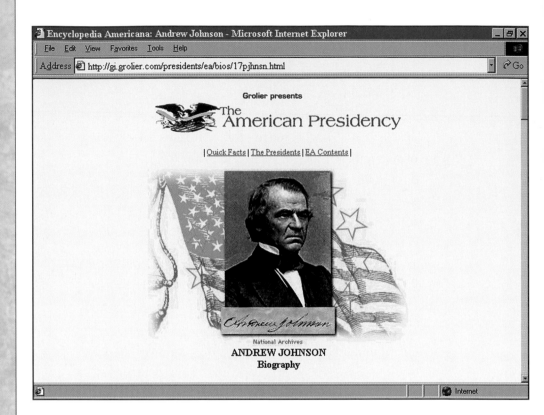

▲ Andrew Johnson became president upon Abraham
Lincoln's assassination.

Radical Republicans. Garfield's support ended when
Johnson vetoed a bill to extend the operation of a federal
agency known as the Freedmen's Bureau.

The Freedmen's Bureau protected the rights of slaves
who had been freed by the Emancipation Proclamation.
The agency assisted freed slaves by providing them with
jobs, land, education, and medical services.

In the midterm elections of 1866, Garfield actively and
vigorously opposed President Johnson. Johnson campaigned
for congressional candidates who favored his lenient plan of
reconstruction. Johnson's plan called for the Southern states

to be quickly readmitted to the Union without punishment. Garfield and other Radical Republicans wanted to treat the South like a conquered nation.

The Radical Republicans won an overwhelming victory. Their power struggle ended with Johnson undergoing an impeachment trial in the Senate. Johnson came within one vote of being impeached, or removed from office. Garfield was disappointed by Johnson's acquittal. During the late 1860s, however, Garfield became more moderate.[2]

In 1868, Garfield unenthusiastically supported the former Union army commander Ulysses S. Grant for president. Grant was twice elected president. During Grant's two terms (1869–77), Garfield became one of the major Republican congressional leaders. Unfortunately, Grant's presidency was undermined by corrupt officials in his administration.

The Crédit Mobilier Scandal

Some of the scandals of the Grant administration plagued Garfield, too. The Crédit Mobilier scandal was the first to affect him. The Crédit Mobilier was a construction company formed in 1864 by shareholders in the Union Pacific Railroad. The Union Pacific was handling the construction of the western part of the transcontinental railroad.

Actual construction costs for building the railroad ranged from $16,000 a mile in flat terrain to $50,000 a mile in mountainous areas. The Crédit Mobilier company charged the Union Pacific Railroad $42,000 to $96,000 a mile. The railroad had to borrow money from Congress, which was subsidizing the construction, to pay for almost $20 million in cost overruns. That money was divided among seven executives of Crédit Mobilier.

To prevent a congressional investigation, the executives set aside 160 shares of stock to sell to influential

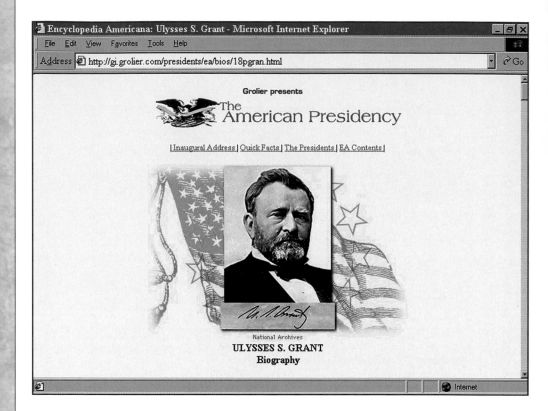

▲ *Ulysses S. Grant, though a remarkable commander in the Civil War, did not fare as well while president.*

congressmen. The stock was selling on the open market for $400 to $500 a share, but favored congressmen were able to buy it for $100 a share.

Eventually, a list of those congressmen was made public. Garfield's name was on it. He was accused of taking ten shares of the stock and a loan of around $300. Garfield testified before a congressional committee, denying any wrongdoing. The committee found no evidence that Garfield had ever owned any Crédit Mobilier stock. They also found no evidence that the loan had ever influenced Garfield's vote. Still, Garfield had to constantly explain and defend his involvement to the voters of his district.

The "Salary Grab" Act

In February 1873, Garfield found himself involved in another congressional controversy. The Forty-second Congress voted to increase its own salary by 50 percent. The raise increased congressional salaries from $5,000 to $7,500 a year, a huge amount for the time. And the raise included pay for the previous two years, to the start of the session in March 1871. Garfield had opposed the measure, but it got buried inside, or became part of, a larger appropriations bill. As the chair of the House Appropriations Committee, Garfield voted for that bill.

The highly unpopular law was quickly labeled the "salary grab." It did more damage to Garfield's reputation than the Crédit Mobilier scandal. Republican conventions at three different counties in his district called for Garfield's resignation.

A stunned and bewildered Garfield decided to fight back. He wrote in his diary, "I do not propose to be killed off without being consulted on the subject."[3] Garfield returned his salary increase to the U.S. Treasury Department. Ohio newspapers soon reported that symbolic gesture. He wrote letters and a pamphlet detailing his side of the story in the Crédit Mobilier scandal and the salary grab.

In November 1874, Garfield was reelected to a seventh term in the House of Representatives. He received almost sixty-five hundred fewer votes than he had in 1872, but he was satisfied. He had cleared his name and regained the voters' trust. In 1876, Garfield became the Republican minority leader. That same year, President Grant declined to seek a third term.

▶ Hayes-Tilden Controversy

The presidential election of 1876 was one of the most hotly contested and controversial of any in American political history. Governor Rutherford B. Hayes of Ohio was the Republican candidate. New York's governor, Samuel J. Tilden, was the Democratic candidate. Tilden had more popular votes, but neither candidate had a majority of electoral votes, which ultimately decide the winner in a presidential election. Tilden led with 184 electoral votes to 166, but he needed 185 to win.

Following two disputed recounts, Congress established an Electoral Commission to settle the matter. The commission was made up of eight Republicans (Garfield among them) and seven Democrats. The commission voted strictly along party lines. By an 8 to 7 vote, it declared Hayes the winner.

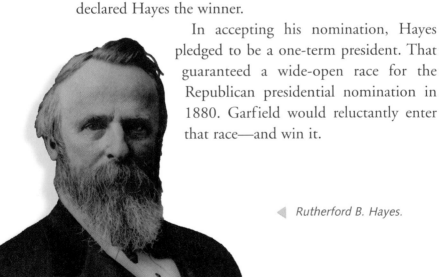

In accepting his nomination, Hayes pledged to be a one-term president. That guaranteed a wide-open race for the Republican presidential nomination in 1880. Garfield would reluctantly enter that race—and win it.

◀ *Rutherford B. Hayes.*

Chapter 6 ▶

Candidate and President-Elect, 1880

During the administration of Rutherford B. Hayes, James Garfield was the minority leader of the House of Representatives, and as such, the most influential Republican in that body. In January of 1880, Garfield was elected to the U.S. Senate. The strong support of Treasury Secretary John Sherman helped Garfield to get elected. In return, Sherman asked Garfield to support him for the Republican presidential nomination. Garfield was happy to help someone who had helped him.

▶ Republican National Convention of 1880

A deeply divided Republican Party met in Chicago for the Republican National Convention of 1880. New York senator Roscoe Conkling led the party's conservatives, known as Stalwarts. The Stalwarts wanted to nominate ex-President Grant. Senator Blaine and Treasury Secretary Sherman were supported by the more moderate Republicans known as Half-Breeds. The Half-Breeds had not settled on either candidate, but they were opposed to Grant. At the convention, Garfield was head of the Rules Committee and the leader of the Sherman forces.

Balloting began after Grant, Blaine, and Sherman were formally submitted as candidates. Grant led in the early balloting. But by the thirty-third ballot, the convention was still deadlocked. To break the deadlock on the thirty-sixth ballot, the Half-Breed backers of Blaine and Sherman decided to back Garfield. Garfield, who had not even

been a candidate at the start of the convention, became his party's nominee, with 399 votes.

The Nominee

Hoping to unify the party, Garfield decided to offer the vice-presidential nomination to one of the Stalwarts. He chose Chester A. Arthur, a New York politician who had never run for elective office. Arthur was honored to accept the nomination.

The Democrats chose Winfield S. Hancock as their presidential candidate. Hancock, a West Point graduate, had a distinguished military record for his service in the Mexican-American War and the Civil War.

A "Front Porch" Campaign

The election of 1880 generated little excitement. The major difference between the parties was in their position on tariffs, or taxes on imported goods. The Republicans favored a high tariff to protect American manufacturers while the Democrats favored a tax simply for raising revenue.

Garfield conducted a leisurely campaign. Instead of hitting the campaign trail, he let the voters come to him. This particular style of campaigning was called a "front porch" campaign. Garfield stayed at his home in Mentor, Ohio. There he greeted

Chester A. Arthur, Garfield's vice president.

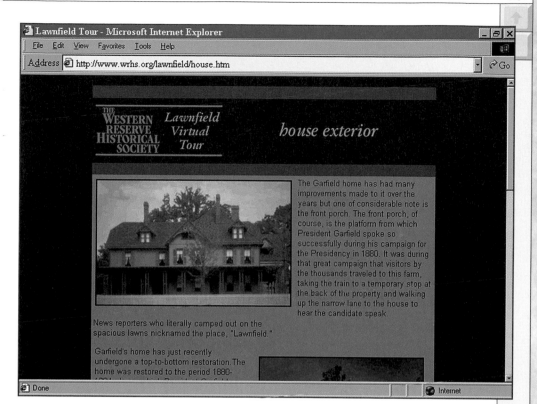

Lawnfield Tour - Microsoft Internet Explorer

File   Edit   View   Favorites   Tools   Help

Address http://www.wrhs.org/lawnfield/house.htm   Go

THE
WESTERN
RESERVE
HISTORICAL
SOCIETY

Lawnfield Virtual Tour

house exterior

The Garfield home has had many improvements made to it over the years but one of considerable note is the front porch. The front porch, of course, is the platform from which President Garfield spoke so successfully during his campaign for the Presidency in 1880. It was during that great campaign that visitors by the thousands traveled to this farm, taking the train to a temporary stop at the back of the property and walking up the narrow lane to the house to hear the candidate speak.

News reporters who literally camped out on the spacious lawns nicknamed the place, "Lawnfield."

Garfield's home has just recently undergone a top-to-bottom restoration. The home was restored to the period 1880-

Done   Internet

▲ *Garfield spoke from his front porch at Lawnfield during the presidential campaign of 1880.*

delegations of supporters while other prominent Republicans made speeches on his behalf.

In the November election, Garfield barely won the popular vote. There were some 9 million votes cast, and Garfield got only about two thousand more votes than Hancock. The electoral vote was not as close. Both candidates carried nineteen states, but Garfield won more of the heavily populated states. He had a margin of 59 electoral votes—214 to 155.

After the election, Garfield resigned his seat in the House. He also resigned as senator-elect from Ohio. Then he concentrated on choosing his cabinet.

▶ **Cabinet Posts and Political Patronage**

Picking cabinet members was a difficult task. Garfield wanted to please both the Stalwarts and the Half-Breeds, and also he knew it was necessary that all regions of the country be represented. His first choice was one of several that would anger Roscoe Conkling and the other Stalwarts. Garfield named his old congressional colleague and friend James G. Blaine as secretary of state. Conkling then demanded the right to name the secretary of the treasury. Garfield refused. Thomas L. James from New York, whom Garfield appointed postmaster general, was the only Stalwart named to a cabinet post. Conkling took issue with James's appointment because he had not been consulted about it. Conkling chose to sulk and call Garfield a traitor to the party, but Garfield did not back down.

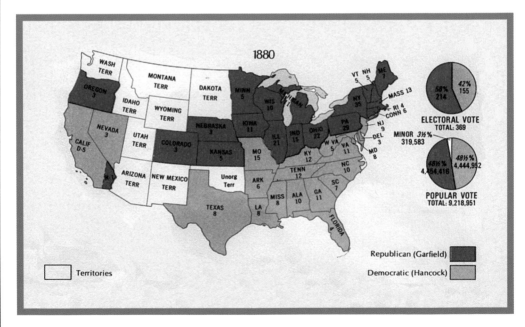

▲ This map shows the results of the presidential election of 1880.

CONKLING, Roscoe (1829-1888) Biographical Information - Microsoft Internet Explorer

File Edit View Favorites Tools Help

Address http://bioguide.congress.gov/scripts/biodisplay.pl?index=C000681

Biographical Directory
of the
United States Congress

1774 - Present

★ Biography
★ Research Collections
★ Bibliography
★ New Search
★ House History Page
★ Senate History Page
★ Copyright Information

CONKLING, Roscoe, 1829-1888

Senate Years of Service: 1867-1881
Party: Republican

Library of Congress

CONKLING, Roscoe, (son of Alfred Conkling and brother of Frederick Augustus Conkling), a Representative and a Senator from New York; born in Albany, N.Y., October 30, 1829; moved with his parents to Auburn, N.Y., in 1839; completed an academic course; studied law; was admitted to the bar in 1850 and commenced practice in Utica, N.Y.; district attorney for Oneida County in 1850; mayor of Utica 1858; elected as a Republican to the Thirty-sixth and Thirty-seventh Congresses (March 4, 1859-March 3, 1863); chairman, Committee on District of Columbia (Thirty-seventh Congress); unsuccessful candidate in 1862 for reelection; elected to the Thirty-ninth and Fortieth Congresses and served from March 4, 1865, until he resigned to become Senator, effective March 4, 1867; elected in 1867 as a Republican to the United States Senate; reelected in 1873 and again in 1879 and served from March 4, 1867, until May 16, 1881, when he resigned as a protest against the federal appointments made in New York State; was an unsuccessful candidate for reelection to the United States Senate to fill the vacancy caused by his own resignation;

Done   Internet

▲ *Senator Roscoe Conkling, head of the Stalwarts, a group within the Republican Party, opposed many of Garfield's decisions.*

Squabbles over political appointments quickly ended any feelings of party unity. Garfield was besieged by friends and foes alike seeking government positions, and he and Conkling battled over patronage. Ultimately, Garfield won when the Senate confirmed William H. Robertson as his choice for collector of the Port of New York. In protest, Conkling resigned from the Senate, ending his political career and his control of the Stalwarts. However, he remained a close friend and mentor of Vice President Arthur.

Chapter 7

President Garfield, 1881

On March 4, 1881, James A. Garfield was inaugurated as America's twentieth president. In his inaugural address, he called the uplifting of black slaves to full citizenship "the most important political change we have known since the adoption of the Constitution. . . ."[1] Garfield pledged to protect and defend the rights of freed slaves, particularly the right to vote. He ended by endorsing civil service reform to replace the spoils system. This system rewarded unqualified party workers with government jobs. Garfield insisted that ". . . offices were created, not for the benefit of incumbents or their supporters, but for the service of the Government."[2]

▶ The Star Route Scandal

Shortly after taking office, Garfield asked Postmaster General Thomas L. James to investigate corruption charges in the post office. James found evidence of widespread fraud in the awarding of mail delivery contracts. There was evidence of bribery by some of Garfield's fellow Republicans. Although there were no convictions, Second Assistant Postmaster General Thomas Brady and others involved in the scandal were forced to resign.

The resignations brought about by the so-called Star Route scandal increased the outcry for civil service reform. The greatest outcry for reforming the system, however, would not come until after President James A. Garfield was assassinated.

▶ Garfield's Assassin

Charles J. Guiteau was a mentally unstable drifter. He got involved in politics after failing to make a living as a lawyer and a bill collector. At the Republican National Convention in 1880, Guiteau wrote a campaign speech for Garfield, but Garfield never used it. Still, Guiteau printed copies of the speech and passed them out at political meetings. When Garfield won the nomination, Guiteau believed he was responsible for the victory.

Guiteau visited the White House a number of times to demand a federal appointment, but each time he was

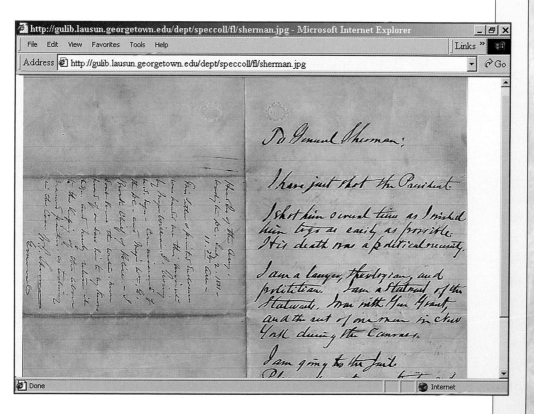

▲ This letter was written by Charles Guiteau to General William Tecumseh Sherman in July 1881. In it, Guiteau writes that he has just shot the president. Guiteau referred to Garfield's death as a "political necessity."

43

turned down. He decided to get his revenge by killing Garfield. He stalked the president for three weeks and was within firing range of him at least three times before backing down. But on the morning of July 2, 1881, he found his target. Guiteau shot Garfield in the waiting room of the Baltimore and Potomac Railroad Station in Washington, D.C. Guiteau was arrested immediately. Garfield lingered between life and death until September 19, when he died in Elberon, New Jersey, where he had been moved earlier in the month. Chester A. Arthur, the vice president, became president upon Garfield's death. On June 30, 1882, Charles Guiteau was hanged for murdering the president of the United States.

▶ Garfield's Legacy

The news that the president was shot by a disappointed office seeker sparked voters' demands for civil service reform. Outrage over Garfield's death spurred Congress to pass the Pendleton Act in 1883. This law provided for open, competitive exams for jobs classified as civil service positions. It would become the greatest legacy of Garfield's brief administration.

Because James A. Garfield served as president for only two hundred days, historians do not rank him with or compare him to other presidents. Yet during his brief term, he showed a willingness to assert the power of the presidency. His showdown with Conkling and the Stalwarts is evidence of that. Also, he was not afraid to root out corruption, even when it meant going after fellow Republicans, as seen in his pursuit of the truth in the Star Route scandal. However briefly he served, Garfield demonstrated considerable potential as president.[3]

Chapter Notes

Chapter 1. Fighting for His Life, 1881

1. Margaret Leech and Harry J. Brown, *The Garfield Orbit* (New York: Harper & Row, 1978), p. 244.

2. Allan Peskin, *Garfield* (Kent, Ohio: The Kent State University Press, 1978), p. 597.

3. Ibid.

4. Ibid., p. 598.

5. John A. Garraty and Mark C. Carnes, *American National Biography* (New York: Oxford University Press, 1999), vol. 2, p. 499.

6. Peskin, p. 606.

7. Theodore C. Smith, *The Life and Letters of James Abram Garfield* (New Haven, Conn.: Yale University Press, 1925), p. 1200.

Chapter 2. The Early Years, 1831–1858

1. William A. DeGregorio, *The Complete Book of U.S. Presidents* (New York: Wings Books, 1997), p. 295.

2. Allan Peskin, *Garfield* (Kent, Ohio: The Kent State University Press, 1978), p. 47.

3. Philip B. Kunhardt, Jr., Philip B. Kunhardt III, and Peter W. Kunhardt, *The American President* (New York: Riverhead Books, 1999), p. 59.

Chapter 3. Politician and Legislator, 1859–1861

1. Allan Peskin, *Garfield* (Kent, Ohio: The Kent State University Press, 1978), p. 75.

2. Philip B. Kunhardt, Jr., Philip B. Kunhardt III, and Peter W. Kunhardt, *The American President* (New York: Riverhead Books, 1999), p. 63.

3. Peskin, p. 77.

4. Ibid.

5. Ibid., p. 79.

Chapter 4. A Talented Union Officer, 1861–1863

1. Allan Peskin, *Garfield* (Kent, Ohio: The Kent State University Press, 1978), p. 84.

2. John A. Garraty and Mark C. Carnes, *American National Biography* (New York: Oxford University Press, 1999), vol. 8, p. 715.

Chapter 5. Congressman Garfield, 1863–1880

1. Edwin P. Hoyt, *James A. Garfield* (Chicago: Reilly and Lee, 1964), p. 81.

2. John A. Garraty and Mark C. Carnes, *American National Biography* (New York: Oxford University Press, 1999), vol. 8, p. 715.

3. Allan Peskin, *Garfield* (Kent, Ohio: The Kent State University Press, 1978), p. 368.

Chapter 7. President Garfield, 1881

1. *Inaugural Addresses of the Presidents of the United States* (Washington, D.C.: U.S. Government Printing Office, 1989), p. 163.

2. Ibid., p. 168.

3. John A. Garraty and Mark C. Carnes, *American National Biography* (New York: Oxford University Press, 1999), vol. 8, p. 716.

Further Reading

Alger, Horatio, Jr. *From Canal Boy to President, or the Boyhood & Manhood of James A. Garfield.* New York: Eighteen Hundred Seventy-Three Press, 2000.

Brown, Fern G. *James A. Garfield: 20th President of the United States.* Ada, Okla.: Garrett Educational Corporation, 1990.

DeGregorio, William A. *The Complete Book of U.S. Presidents.* New York: Wings Books, 1997.

Doenecke, Justus D. *The Presidencies of James A. Garfield & Chester A. Arthur.* Lawrence: The Regents Press of Kansas, 1981.

Hendrik, Booraem V. *The Road to Respectability: James A. Garfield and His World, 1844–1852.* Cranbury, N.J.: Bucknell University Press, 1988.

Joseph, Paul. *James A. Garfield.* Edina, Minn.: ABDO Publishing Company, 2000.

Leech, Margaret and Harry J. Brown. *The Garfield Orbit.* New York: Harper & Row, 1978.

Lillegard, Dee. *James A. Garfield.* Danbury, Conn.: Children's Press, 1987.

Peskin, Allan. *Garfield.* Kent, Ohio: The Kent State University Press, 1978.

Smith, Theodore C. *The Life and Letters of James Abram Garfield.* New Haven, Conn.: Yale University Press, 1925.

Steins, Richard. *Hayes, Garfield, Arthur, & Cleveland.* Vero Beach, Fla.: Rourke Corporation, 1996.

Young, Jeff C. *The Fathers of American Presidents.* Jefferson, N.C.: McFarland and Co. Publishers, 1997.

Ziff, Marsha. *Reconstruction Following the Civil War in American History.* Berkeley Heights, N.J.: Enslow Publishers, Inc., 1999.

Index